Aberdyfi Past and Present

Aberdyfi
Past and Present

Hugh M. Lewis M.B.E.

By the same author:

Aberdyfi in Retrospect (1968)
Aberdyfi Legends and History (1969)
The Story of Aberdyfi (1972)
A Riverside Story (1974)
Aberdyfi: A Glimpse of the Past (1975)
The Bells of Aberdyfi (1982)
Aberdyfi: Portrait of a Village (1985)
Pages of Time (1989)
Time and Tide (1992)
Aberdyfi Through my Window (1994)
Aberdyfi: A Chronicle through the Centuries (1997)
Aberdyfi: The Past Recalled (2001)

Praise for H.M. Lewis's Publications:
The late Professor Emeritus Wyndraeth H. Morris-Jones of the University of London:
"Hugh Lewis is a notable historian of record"

Of Aberdyfi Through My Window: "Of a markedly special quality, most finely written. I consider that this is writing of distinctively Welsh local history at its best."

First impression: 2003

Cover: Ceri Jones
ISBN: 0 86243 652 4

Dinas is an imprint of Y Lolfa

y Lolfa

Printed and published in Wales
by Y Lolfa Cyf., Talybont, Ceredigion SY24 5AP
e-mail ylolfa@ylolfa.com
website www.ylolfa.com
tel. (01970) 832 304

INTRODUCTION

Old photographs possess a unique power of recalling memories of things long forgotten. They are our magical links to the past. Now that I have reached my ninety-third year, I find that our way of life is much changed.

I was born into a way of life that was so different. Now that I have time to reflect on the great changes that have taken place, photographs provide me with an invaluable insight into aspects of local life which regretfully are now disappearing.

Hugh M.Lewis

ACKNOWLEDGEMENTS

I have received much support and enouragement
in my literary efforts from a number of people,
but would particularly like to mention
Dr A. Armstrong and Mr G. Edwards B.A.,
who have both been most helpful.

Hugh Meirion Lewis, MBE

4th September 1910 – 22nd April 2003

CONTENTS

A Peaceful Haven

ONE OF MY FAVOURITE WELSH POEMS

Yng nghanol mor fy mywyd i
Y mae ynys fechan braf
Ac yno weithiau gyda'r nos
Yng nghwch fy hiraeth af
Does ond myfi a thonnau'r mor
Wyr am y Sanctaidd dir

MY ENGLISH TRANSLATION

A beautiful small island exists
In the centre of the sea of my life
Its magic draws me, often at night
On a journey away from all strife
Only the restless waves of the sea
Share this sacred place with me

This short poem tells of an island of the imagination which exists in the minds of many people. It is an idyllic place which is waiting for you and you alone. It is where you can go with your thoughts, your wishes, your ideas and your longings.

It can be anywhere that you wish to make it; a wood, a street, a path, or a place where you have spent happy moments perhaps in childhood. It can create its own time and space for tranquillity and reflection.

Sometimes to get there you can travel over calm waters. At other times, when the sea of life is rough and stormy with events hard to bear, you may have to fight hard to reach your peaceful haven.

When you finally arrive all will be calm, quiet and restful. It will give you everything that you want. It is a place we all need.

Aberdyfi has provided me with a peaceful haven with all the time to reflect in the most perfect and tranquil of settings. It has its own magic which draws me. It will always be my home, a place of the imagination.

Hugh M. Lewis M.B.E.

1. THE VILLAGE

THE VILLAGE SQUARE

In 1867, several temperance lodging houses opened up in the village and the best known was the Victoria Temperance Hotel, which occupied a corner site facing Copper Hill Street and the Village Square. The name of this hotel was changed to Gwalia (picture 1), which is a Welsh name for Wales. When this hotel closed the site was taken over by a chemist shop. This was located next to the village bakehouse, where villagers took their bread to be baked.

In front of these buildings was the village water pump, while overlooking the square is the Wesleyan Methodist Chapel. On the other side of the square was a grocer's shop (picture 2) and to complete this

1. Gwalia Temperance Hotel

ABERDOVEY

(COPPERHILL STREET)

Grocery & Provision

Establishment.

Also Branch at Glanaber House, Penhelig.

AGENT for Nectar, Mazawattee, Dwyryd, and Horniman's Teas. Fresh Roasted Coffee. Huntley and Palmer's, Peek Frean, and Macfarlane's Biscuits and Cakes. Beach's, Chivers', Hartley's, and Keiller's Jams and Marmalade. Home-cured Hams and Bacon, Harris' Smoked.

Daily Supplies of Fresh Butter, Eggs, and Cream.

Quality of all goods guaranteed. Visitors are invited to apply for Price List.

House Agent (by License) for the District.

List of Houses and Apartments sent on application, also Building Plots and Houses for Sale.

Proprietor - - E. L. ROWLANDS.

2. Grocer's shop known as Liverpool House

picture of the busy square in the centre of the village, there was a greengrocer's shop (picture 3). All traffic to the hillside houses, several farms and up and down Copper Hill Street and Church Street has to go through this area. Today, the Wesleyan Chapel (see page 76) still dominates the area.

ROYAL HOUSE

Royal House, in Sea View Terrace, was built in 1615. It is one of the oldest houses in the village. Once called Ty Mawr (The Great House), it was probably a house of refreshment for ferry passengers crossing the River Dyfi. The building extended from

3. The Corner of the Village Square today

1. Royal Raven

the corner of Copper Hill Street to an opening on the western end adjoining London House. This gave access to the stables at the rear, where horses were kept for the stagecoach and other vehicles. In 1800, the name of the hostelry was changed and Ty Mawr became known as the Raven Inn, probably because the crest of the Corbet family of Ynysmaengwyn, who owned most of the village, bore a raven.

Following an overnight stay by a princess of the Stuart royal family, who was returning home from a visit to Ynysmaengwyn but was prevented by wind and tide from crossing by the ferry, the prefix Royal was added and the hotel became known as the Royal Raven (picture 1).

A part of the building was once used as a ship's chandlery and it was appropriately called the Store House, as it supplied gear for the fast-growing shipping industry.

A beam bearing the carved date 1645 was uncovered whilst the old tavern was being converted into a modern shop (picture 2). During further changes, a rain pipe was discovered bearing the inscribed date 1871 (picture 3).

3. Rain pipe with date, inscribed 1871

2. Beam bearing carved date 1645

4. *Royal House as it is today*

VILLAGE WORKSHOPS

At the turn of the century, there were several small workshops in the village, including a blacksmith, cobbler, tailor, barber, printer and a tannery.

A tailor lived in the ground floor of Glanaber, Terrace Road, and a printer occupied part of the old Lifeboat House. In 1978, the last of the small workshops, a family-owned bakery, was closed. One of the last surviving buildings of this type can still be seen in Church Street and has been recently renovated (picture 1).

1. A small workshop in Church Street - 1900

On a site in Penhelig there was a blacksmith's shop (or smithy as it was known). It was equipped for shoeing horses and making hoops for cart wheels. In addition, it produced ironwork of all kinds for the growing shipping industry and for carrying out general repairs. It was not only a place of intense work but also where the older men met to discuss local affairs (picture 2).

When the motor car appeared on the roads, the days of the blacksmith were numbered. Eventually, the old smithy was converted into lock-up garages (pictures 3 and 4).

2. The village blacksmith in Penhelig - 1880

3. *Blacksmith's shop converted into lock-up garages – 1935*

4. *The lock-up garages today*

THE VILLAGE WATER SUPPLY

In the early days, few cottages had a water supply and so water for all needs had to be carried from the village pump (picture 1) or from two natural springs at each end of the village. Toilet facilities were primitive but there were dry outside closets. It is surprising how large families were reared under such conditions, but somehow people happily survived.

In 1898, a new water supply scheme to replace the old village pump was inaugurated. This included building a reservoir in the hills behind the village near Crychnant Farm. It was of open construction, twenty-one feet deep and with a capacity of three million gallons (picture 2). Water mains were laid, and houses connected.

1. The village pump in the square – 1880

2. Reservoir in the mountains –

VILLAGE TRANSPORT

With the development of the motor industry, the first motor car made its appearance in Aberdyfi (picture 1). It conjured up an air of adventure, with plenty of noise, smoke, fumes and much snorting and vibrating. The starting handle was an essential piece of equipment, while windscreen wipers had not yet been invented. A large rubber bulb blew the horn to warn all and sundry of the car's erratic journey along the narrow Aberdyfi roads.

1. An early motor car

The railway station was some way out of the village and it was not at all conveniently sited for elderly travellers. A horse-drawn bus used to ply regularly to and fro between the station and the village. The passenger door of this bus was at the rear and it had a protruding step (picture 2).

2. The horse-bus

A single track railway and an old turnpike road were our links with the outside world. The village carrier delivered parcels, crates and boxes from the railway station to the shops (picture 3).

3. The village carrier

SEA VIEW TERRACE (FACING EAST)

In 1834, Aberdyfi was a small fishing village. In this first picture of Sea View Terrace (picture 1), a fishing smack can be seen on the foreshore with fishing nets hung to dry on poles. The cottages of the terrace facing the river have thatched roofs, while the wattle walls were supported by large stones placed to act as buttresses.

1. Fishing smack and nets hung to dry on foreshore

By 1900 (picture 2), various new structures can be seen, including St Peter's Church, the Methodist Chapel and the Britannia Inn. In addition, there are railings along the promenade placed to protect pedestrians from the main road. This view is little changed today (picture 3).

2. Sea View Terrace about 1900

3. Sea View Terrace today

1. Sea View Terrace about 1900 before the promenade was built

SEA VIEW TERRACE (FACING WEST)

In the first view of Sea View Terrace (picture 1), taken about 1900, there is no promenade and drying fishing nets can be seen opposite the Britannia Inn. The Midland and National Westminster Banks have not yet opened and coal trucks can be seen on the wharf. The railings on the promenade can be seen on the road side only. Gas lighting is evident but there are no cars.

2. Later view of Sea View Terrace showing the promenade

THE LITERARY INSTITUTE

In 1842, a new religious sect called the Plymouth Brethren was holding its meetings in a chapel on the seashore. It was known as the Bath House, an appropriate name, as their teachings required that they made frequent use of total immersion.

In 1882, the chapel became vacant. It was acquired by the inhabitants of Aberdyfi to provide premises for meetings, lectures, classes, a library and a reading room. It also catered for other leisure-time activities, such as billiards, snooker, chess and draughts, with the object of improving the quality of life in the village. The Institute is still used for local functions, including meetings of the Aberdyfi Community Council.

GLANDYFI TERRACE

The first photograph was probably taken on a Sunday around 1900. The boys are all wearing caps and long trousers, which were worn on Sundays only. Girls are obviously wearing their neat Sunday-best clothes.

1. Glandyfi Terrace about 1900

The picture shows the terrace known as Glandyfi once called the Turnpike Road. The gap in the sea front houses between 4 Bodfor Terrace and 1 Glandyfi Terrace was the site of one of the many ship-building yards in Aberdyfi. A sloop, 'Mountain Maid', was built here in 1851.

In the second photograph, the gap has been filled with new houses.

2. Later view of Glandyfi Terrace (Note the railway trucks on the sea shore)

3. Glandyfi Terrace today

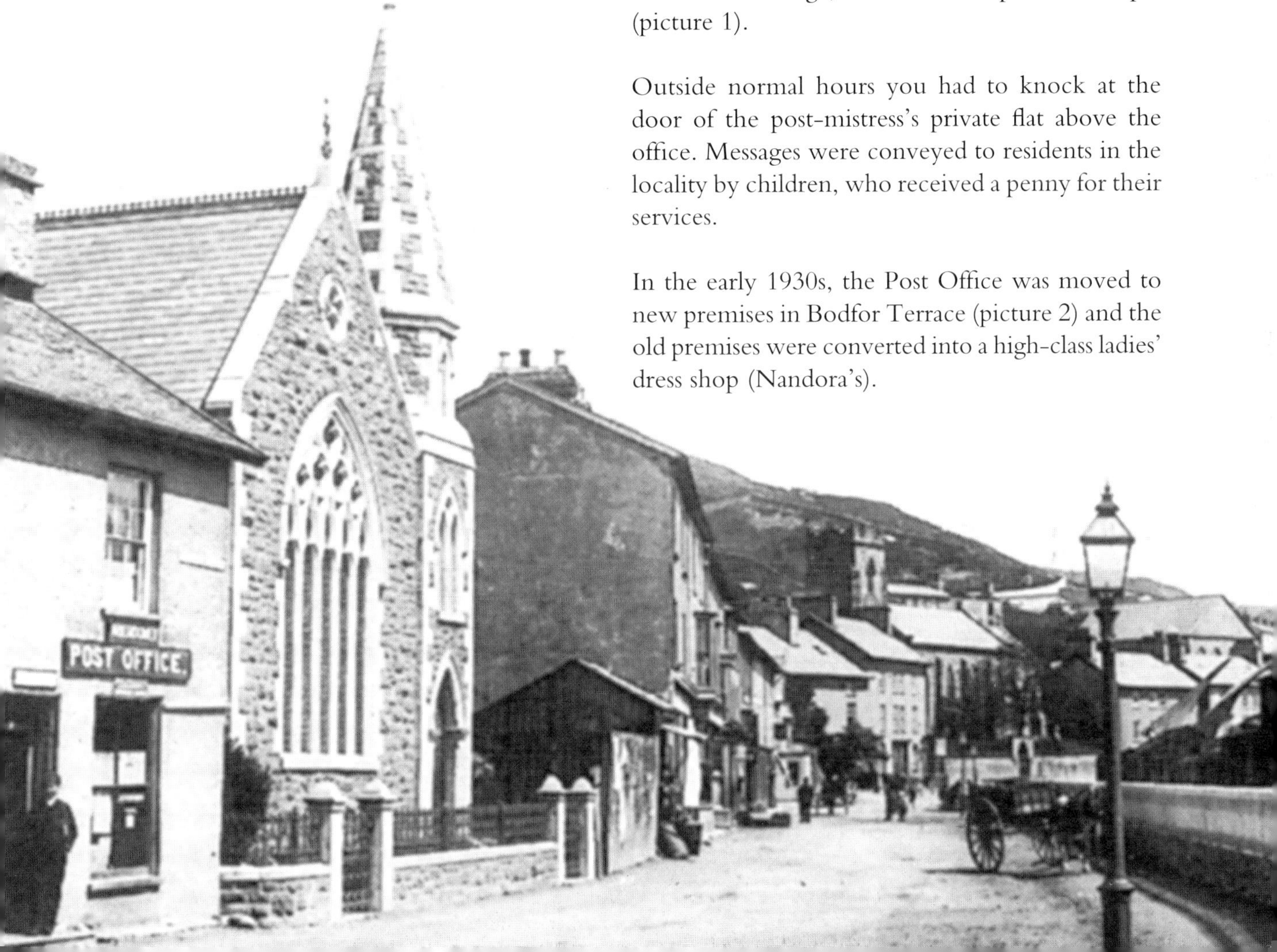

1. *The original post office*

THE POST OFFICE

Telephones were scarce in the village and public call boxes completely lacking. If a telephone was needed, which was not often, a visit had to be made to the village Post Office. This was situated in the centre of the village, next to the Independent Chapel (picture 1).

Outside normal hours you had to knock at the door of the post-mistress's private flat above the office. Messages were conveyed to residents in the locality by children, who received a penny for their services.

In the early 1930s, the Post Office was moved to new premises in Bodfor Terrace (picture 2) and the old premises were converted into a high-class ladies' dress shop (Nandora's).

2. The new post office

THE MAIN CAR PARK

Before 1870, the foreshore in front of Bodfor Terrace and Glandyfi Terrace was separated from the main road by a low wall (picture 1). This was built to stop pedestrians straying onto the railway lines which connected the wharf and jetty with the main railway.

With the decline in shipping, the harbour had become neglected and untidy so these lines were removed. The old wall was demolished in 1988 and the main road widened, while a new wall with a promenade was built on the beach. In addition, a much needed car park was laid out in this area (picture 2). It has recently been expanded to accommodate holiday traffic (picture 3).

1. Railway lines along the shore
(Note the horse-drawn cab, no pavements on main road)

2. The new car park

3. The latest car park

MYNYDD ISAF AND MAESNEWYDD

Prior to 1950, the upper part of Copper Hill Street ended at a gate leading to Tŷ-Newydd fields. Picture 1 shows the empty Tŷ-Newydd fields prior to development. It was here that a Council estate called Maesnewydd was built (picture 2), while the nearby Balkan Hill fields were developed as the Mynydd Isaf estate in 1989 (picture 3).

1. The Tŷ-Newydd fields showing the gate at the top of Copper Hill Street and the boundary of Tŷ-Newydd

2. The development of Maesnewydd

3. Balkan Hill fields

2. PENHELIG

THE LIFEBOAT HOUSE

In 1884, it was thought necessary to find a new and more convenient building to accommodate a larger lifeboat. A site in Penhelig was purchased for £150 and a new boathouse built at a cost of £400. The boat had to be taken along the main road for launching onto the river at a convenient point (picture 1).

1. The new lifeboat house in Penhelig

In 1903, a new slipway was constructed opposite the new boathouse at a cost of £300 (picture 2).

The Aberdyfi lifeboat station was closed in 1931 and a small high-speed reserve craft was introduced. The lifeboat house has since been converted into a private dwelling house (picture 3). The official insignia belonging to the old lifeboat house can still be seen on the piers of the new house (picture 4).

2. Launching the boat on the new slipway (1903)

3. Official insignia at the entrance of the lifeboat house

4. The lifeboat house as it is today

TERRACE ROAD (FACING EAST)

'Glanaber', which features in the first photograph, was once occupied by two elderly ladies who dispensed afternoon teas on the ground floor. Later this house was used as a butcher's shop and a tailor's workshop. The two doors which lead to these premises can still be seen today (picture 1).

The area beyond 'Glanaber' was a builder's yard, separated from the main road by a high stone wall. At this date the area on the river side of the road is still undeveloped but an early gas street lamp is visible.

1. Terrace Road showing 'Glanaber'

2. The ship-builder's workshop next to the new lifeboat house

Picture 2 shows a ship-builder's workshop on a site next door to where the lifeboat house would later be built.

In picture 3, the ship-builders' workshop has vanished and a bungalow has been erected on the site. The new lifeboat house can be seen and a public shelter has been erected by the main road. Telegraph poles are appearing in the village. Now a garage has been built on the builder's yard (the stone wall has disappeared) and a grocer's shop stands next to 'Glanaber'. A barber's shop and a fish-and-chip shop have appeared on the scene. Altogether it has become a place of much activity.

3. Garage built on the builder's yard

By the time that picture 4 was taken, the garage has gone and the area has been laid out for a parking place. Now the grocer's shop has vanished, as has the barber's shop. Paul's Hairdressing salon is now a domestic house.

4. Terrace Road as it is today

TERRACE ROAD (FACING WEST)

In 1837 the first lifeboat arrived in Aberdyfi and was housed in a stone building specially built on the beach in Penhelig (picture 1). The west gable-end had a wide doorway through which the boat was taken out on its wheeled carriage. It was then trundled along the village street to one of a number of convenient places giving easy access to the river.

1. 'Traeth Dyfi', once Aberdyfi's first lifeboat house

The row of cottages opposite was known as Lifeboat Terrace. The building at the top of this terrace was originally a sail-making workshop. It later became a blacksmith's workshop, and later still, a bakehouse supplying bread and cakes to the little shop that occupied the old Lifeboat House. Today, the Lifeboat House has become a dwelling house, and is known as 'Traeth Dyfi'.

2. Lifeboat Terrace

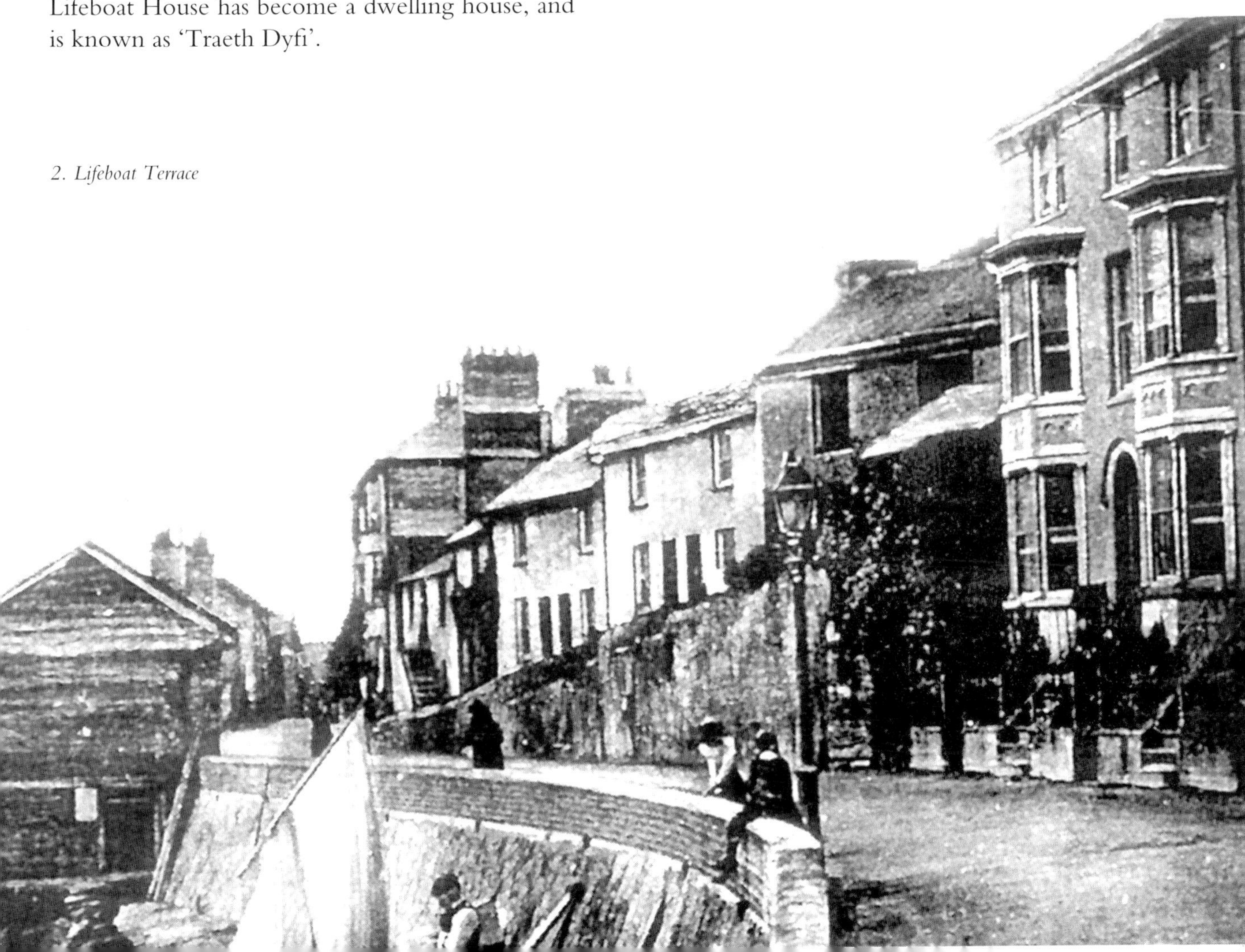

In 1927, a new house was built on the site of the old bakehouse, now known as 'Seacot'. In picture 2, a part of the terrace of houses known as Cliffside and built in 1885, can be seen, as well as the gas street lamps of that period.

3. Terrace Road as it is today

PENHELIG ARMS HOTEL

Penhelig Arms Hotel was built by Captain Humphrey Edwards, probably in 1780 as is indicated in the sign-board above the door in the first photograph. The sign also mentions Edward Davies as the Licensed Retailer of Beers and Spirits. Edward was a relative of Humphrey Edwards. We know that he was born in 1780 and was a native of Pennal. He was master of the 'Glanavon' sailing ship until his retirement. The mariners shown in the picture (1890) are of course of a later generation.

The second photograph shows that there was a garden in the front of the hotel – now a parking area. The bay windows in the frontage were built about 1930. The cottage adjoining the hotel has now been incorporated into the main building, as has the cottage at the other end of the building.

1. The Penhelig Arms Hotel

2. The hotel garden, now a car park

3. The hotel today

THE PENHELIG SHIPYARDS

In 1851 the shipbuilding industry was booming in Aberdyfi. There were seven shipyards in Penhelig alone. Ships of all sizes including 45 sailing ships were built there between 1846 and 1880. However, when the Cambrian Railway reached the village and started tunneling, shipbuilding activity swiftly came to an end.

The material excavated from the tunnels was dumped on the shore, where the shipbuilders once toiled. Later on, Penhelig Terrace was built on this area of rock waste and the adjacent area was laid out as a park.

1. Penhelig's picturesque cove (1837)

2. Fisherman's cottages in Penhelig

3. The coming of the railway

4. Penhelig shipyard

5. Penhelig Terrace

6. Penhelig Park

THE CHURCH HALL

In 1922, the church authorities decided that a new hall was needed in Aberdyfi to cater for village activities. A fine site was chosen overlooking the estuary in Penhelig.

Ever since known simply as the 'Church Hall', public meetings of all kinds have been held here over the years: concerts, whist drives, dances and political gatherings. Many local organisations including the Women's Institute, the Gardening Club and several youth clubs have used it as their venue. More recently the annual exhibition of the Aberdyfi Art Club has been held here. Indeed, the Church Hall has been at the centre of village life.

With the arrival of Neuadd Dyfi the Church Hall has been less of a focus. In 2001 it was sold by public auction and it has now been converted into a private residence.

The Church Hall

3. PENRHOS

ARDUDWY MILL

In 1881, the Aberdyfi Roller and Flour Mill was built on a site near Ardudwy to the west of the village. Shiploads of grain, barley and wheat for the grinding of flour arrived from Australia, Canada and other distant places. After the grain had been milled, it was loaded into ships for export to various destinations. A private housing estate now occuppies the site where the old mill stood, and is appropriately named Melin Ardudwy (Ardudwy Mill).

1. The Ardudwy Flour Mill (1881)

2. Private housing estate on the site of the Ardudwy Mill

CORBET ARMS HOTEL

When the Turnpike Trust was established in 1775, a road was built to connect Tywyn with Machynlleth. This road went through Happy Valley (Cwm Maethlon). Later, the Turnpike Trust, anticipating the rapid growth of Aberdyfi, built the present coastal road. With the advent of stage-coaches, passengers required lodgings and refreshments, so in 1829 the Corbet Arms Family Hotel was built at the western end of the village (picture 1).

In 1867, to prepare for the expected influx of visitors, the old Corbet Arms Hotel was rebuilt (picture 2). However, there was no immediate rush to the coast and over the years the hotel wore a sad and neglected look. In 1914, the empty Corbet Hotel suffered its final indignity when the whole structure was burned to the ground (picture 3).

1. The first Corbet Arms Hotel in 1829

For many years the site was deserted and derelict and not until 1968 did it regain some of its former glory when the Primary School was transferred here from Pen-y-Bryn.

2. The rebuilt Corbet Arms Hotel in 1867

3. Aftermath of the fire in 1914

THE ABERDYFI GOLF CLUB

It is a little known fact that the first game of golf played in Wales was on the old Aberdyfi common. In 1892 the Aberdyfi Golf Club was formed and the first Club House was built in 1895 to meet the needs of the increasing membership. This building had a circular verandah and had only one storey (picture 1). The first tournament of the new Welsh Golfing Union was held in Aberdyfi in 1895 and the Aberdyfi links have since developed into one of the finest championship courses in Wales.

The old Club House was burnt down in 1908, and a new one was constructed with more spacious accommodation (picture 2).

After the First World War, the Aberdyfi course was greatly improved, with external drainage. These alterations were completed in 1920. Following the Second World War, Aberdyfi hosted the Welsh Professional Championship in 1948 and the Welsh Amateur Championship in 1949.

1. Aberdyfi's original Club House

2. The second Club House

3. Today's Club House

PENRHOS CARAVAN PARK

As holiday caravans were coming to the area in increasing numbers, a vacant area between the railway station and the sand dunes was cleared after the Second World War to accommodate them. The area was levelled and roads were laid and connected to the public services.

There are now a hundred permanent caravans on this site, which has proved very popular, as it is virtually on the seashore and hence ideal for holiday makers. The tents in this picture were used by village lads during the summer months.

2. A later view of the site showing the caravan park

1. Early view of the site showing tents

EDUCATION

With the rapid expansion of the village, and the increase in population, it became necessary to provide young children with the rudiments of education. As there was at the time a close relationship between religion and education, a school was started in the old Methodist chapel in the square. However, it was eventually decided to build a new school on Brynhyfryd. This building, known as the National School, opened its doors in 1854. Education continued smoothly here for many years, until there came a point when Church and Chapel began to disagree on matters of policy. The non-conformists acquired the old Congregational chapel on Pen-y-Bryn, demolishing it, and building

1. The Pen-y-Bryn school

a new school on the site for the Chapel children. This school opened in 1894.

The two schools carried on separately until the 1939-45 war brought an influx of evacuees into the village. The Church, or National School, was allocated to them and their teachers for their use, with all of the village children again occupying the British, or Board School on Pen-y-Bryn (picture 1). When the war ended, and the evacuees returned home, Aberdyfi again had two schools for its own use. It was decided that the youngest children, the infants should attend the British School, whilst the older children should be educated in the National School.

In 1968 a new modern school was built for all the children on the site of the old Corbet ruins in Penrhos (picture 2). Both of the earlier schools are now private residences.

2. The Corbet school

TREFEDDIAN HOTEL

Built in 1904, and standing in an elevated, south-facing position overlooking Cardigan Bay, the Trefeddian Hotel is the largest hotel in this part of Wales. It has been under the ownership of the Cave family since 1920.

The first photograph shows the hotel in 1905, while the increased size of the improved building can be seen in the second, taken about 1925. Trefeddian has always been popular with golfers, situated as it is so conveniently close to the course, and this is obvious from the third picture, taken about 1982.

1. Trefeddian Hotel in 1905

2. The hotel in 1925

3. The hotel in 1982

Recently the hotel has been modernised again, with a new top floor added and all amenities improved. It is now a truly first-class hotel (picture 4).

4. Trefeddian Hotel today

NEUADD DYFI

By the 1920s the chapel vestries and the local schools felt that they were no longer able to accommodate the increasing numbers of people wishing to attend concerts, plays, public meetings and other social events, and that a large hall, specially built for the purpose, was needed.

The first such hall to appear in Aberdyfi was an ex-army building purchased in Oswestry, dismantled and transported to the village. It was erected in Penrhos and was known as the Pavilion. Over the years the Pavilion was used by various organisations including a successful drama society and an orchestra. It also served as a a cinema.

By the 1950s the structure was beginning to deteriorate, and so it was decided to replace it with a new building. This was opened in 1957 and named Neuadd Dyfi. Much of the cost of this building was met by public subscription.

By the end of the century Neuadd Dyfi was again in bad repair, particularly the roof. More and more maintenance was required, and by now the facilities were inadequate. To finance the refurbishment, government grants were applied for and work was started. This entailed levelling the floor, building a new kitchen and changing rooms, providing toilets and a new roof.

Now once again Neuadd Dyfi can take its place at the centre of village life.

ABERDYFI RECREATION GROUND

When the railway company decided to build an embankment practically on the shore and westwards from Bodfor Terrace, an area of land between the mountains and the sea became available for development. The Council decided at an early stage to make this part of Aberdyfi available for recreational purposes, and over the years it has become a pleasant area much frequented by visitors.

1. Village bowlers in their open hut in 1921

There are facilities here for playing tennis, bowls and miniature golf, and there is a full-size football field. I have fond memories of many closely fought contests played out here, and will never forget how in 1934 Aberdyfi won the Welsh Amateur Cup Championship.

The Aberdyfi Bowling Club was formed in 1921 and soon after it was invited to join the Montgomeryshire League. In 1974 the Club became the League Champions.

In 1997, the Bowling Club took over the running of the Recreation Ground from the Council, and proceeded to carry out improvements to the lawns and buildings. The club-house kitchen has been radically altered, while the green and its environs have been upgraded. At long last the Bowling Club has a club-house to be proud of, where they can entertain visiting teams in style.

2. The recreation ground today

3. Tennis, miniature golf and croquet

4. VILLAGE CENTRE

THE CHANGING FACE OF THE VILLAGE CENTRE

The Cambrian Railway wanted to develop Aberdyfi into a port involved in the transportation of slate, livestock, timber, coal, steel rails, railway sleepers and agricultural produce. To facilitate the loading and unloading of ships, the Cambrian Railway in 1882 erected a wharf about 500 feet long and 250 feet wide. Two large buildings were constructed for the storage of grain and other products. In addition, a jetty was built which protruded into the river, so that ships could load and unload, whatever the state of the tide.

Thus, the centre of the village was changed out of all recognition, as was the seashore, where railway lines were laid to connect the wharf and the main line. Mingling with yachts and holiday-makers, the tracks were covered by drifting sand blown by the prevailing westerly winds.

1. The village centre before the wharf and jetty were built in 1882

The wharf was a valuable link to the quarries at Abergynolwyn, via the newly opened Talyllyn Railway. Large quantities of slate were transported to the wharf for shipment. Each year, fifty ships were loading 100 tons per ship to all parts of the world. At the western end of the village, the railway company constructed a large embankment practically on the seashore. This cut off the sea which used to come in as far as the line of the main road.

During the years following the 1914-18 war, there was very little commercial activity in this area. The jetty became deserted and the once busy wharf was used as a coal dump. The men who had sailed to all parts of the world were now ashore, and to earn a livelihood they turned once again to fishing.

2. Activity on the new wharf

3. *The new jetty*

4. *Railway lines stretch along the foreshore*

5. The first railway engine

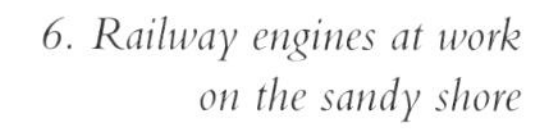

6. Railway engines at work on the sandy shore

7. The structure of the wharf and jetty deteriorated

The Great Western took over from the Cambrian Railway in 1923, but little was done about the harbour and there was very little commercial activity. Over the years, the structure of the wharf and jetty deteriorated steadily and the wharf became dilapidated.

In 1965, following protracted negotiations with British Rail, the whole area was acquired by the Urban District Council. In 1972, they proceeded to develop and improve the area by erecting a new steel-piled wall around the outside of the old timber face. The railway lines were removed and the whole area was transformed into a sea-front garden.

8. and 9. The once-busy wharf used as a coal dump

10. The whole area transformed into sea-front gardens

CATTLE PENS ALONG THE SEA-FRONT

The Aberdyfi jetty had two levels, a higher one for serving boats when the tide was in, and a lower level for when the tide was out. When a boat had docked, one could watch cattle, pigs and horses being driven ashore. They were herded into special pens erected along the front opposite Glandovey Terrace and Bodfor Terrace.

Later a railway line was built to serve the area between the road and the beach. Animals could then be loaded straight onto trucks and driven away.

Cattle pens along the sea front 1872

THE DYFI YACHT CLUB

The Dyfi Sailing Club was formed in 1949 by a group of local people who owned an assortment of dinghies of all shapes and sizes. As interest grew, it became evident that an inexpensive, modern, single-design boat ought to be used by all members and the GP14 was selected as the most suitable. Its sail insignia of a black bell marked an association with the village that had gained national fame with the song 'The Bells of Aberdyfi'. An old air-raid shelter on the sea-front was used as a club room.

1. The Old Sailing Club building, once an air-raid shelter

As part of the development of the old wharf, an area of land was leased by the council to the Club. Here they built a new Club House and changed their name to the Dyfi Yacht Club.

On Whit Monday 1970, there was a large gathering at the new Yacht Club premises. The then chairman of the District Council, Cllr Hugh M. Lewis (one of the small group of locals who had formed the club in 1949) officially opened the new Club House in the 21st year of the Club's formation. The Tywyn Silver Band was in attendance.

2. The new Yacht Club building

THE OUTWARD BOUND SEA SCHOOL

The first Outward Bound Centre was started in Aberdyfi in 1941. Here young people from all walks of life attend residential courses throughout the year (picture 1). The Outward Bound Trust is supported by industry and commerce, and a wide range of outdoor activities take place in the Dyfi estuary and Cader Idris mountain range. There are now many Outward Bound Centres throughout the world.

1. Young sailors with the Outward Bound Sea School (O.B.S.S.)

The two large buildings constructed on the wharf for the storage of grain and other products are now occupied by the Outward Bound (picture 2).

2. O.B.S.S. buildings on the wharf

5. RELIGION

THE FIRST METHODIST CHAPEL

We know that the Calvinistic Methodists had a chapel in Ty-Coch, Nantiesyn in 1796, where they worshipped for twenty-six years. In 1828, however, as the population of the village increased, they built a chapel in New Street which was called 'Tabernacle'. They vacated the old chapel in 1864 for a larger building on the sea front taking the name 'Tabernacle' with them. The old building assumed a new role as the meeting-place for village activities and was known as 'The Assembly Rooms'. The first village school met here in 1847.

Subsequently, the Catholic Church met here in 1931 but later there was a change in its function yet again when the ground floor area was converted into a shopping arcade. The building was now called 'The Market Hall'.

1. Chapel called 'Tabernacle' in New Street

The upper floor was retained as a place for meetings and where local singers and poetry reciters took the stage. It proved to be a good training ground for many promising youngsters and was known as 'The Imperial Hall'.

During the Second World War, the building was used as the headquarters of the Home Guard. Today this building, after a chequered history, is following the nautical tradition of the village as a marine chandler's.

2. The same building converted to a market hall

3. The building as it is today

THE SECOND METHODIST CHAPEL (CALVINISTIC)

In 1859, a powerful religious revival swept through North Wales and the various denominations found their places of worship too small. The Calvinistic Methodists decided to build a new chapel for a congregation of 650 on the sea-front.

Following the 1905 revival, the chapel had a major renovation and a fine pipe organ was installed. It was called 'Tabernacle' and could seat a thousand worshippers. The chapel was used to hold special events including concerts, oratorios and other musical events. Today, the 'Tabernacle' is no longer used as a chapel and has been sold for conversion into flats. This task is now complete.

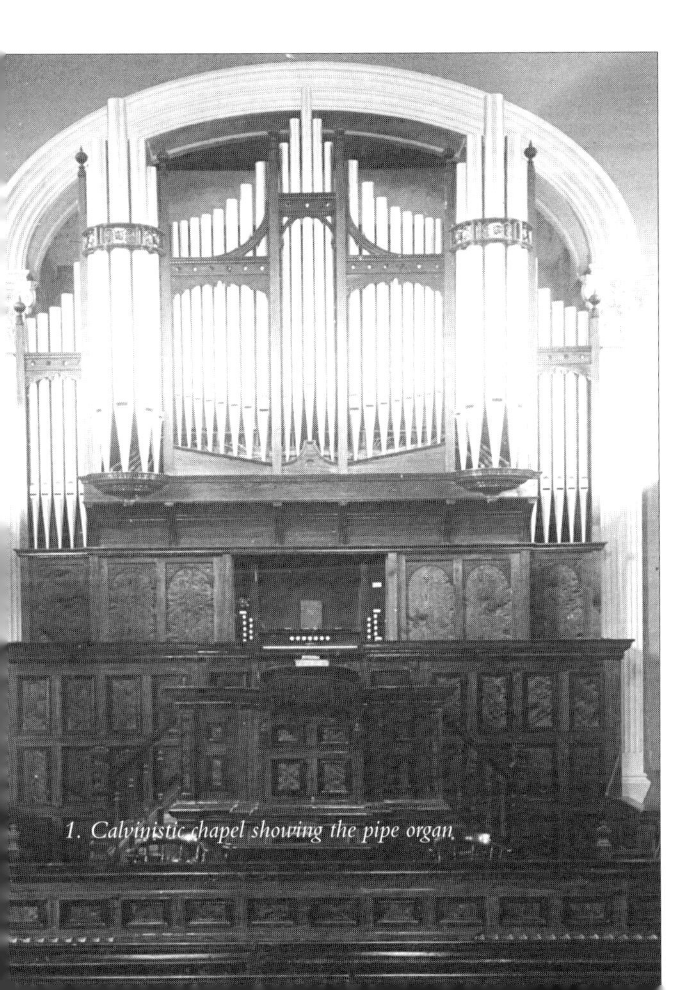

1. Calvinistic chapel showing the pipe organ.

2. Chapel building re-development

1. Original Wesleyan chapel in the square

WESLEYAN METHODIST CHAPEL

The Wesleyan Methodists came to Aberdyfi in 1804. At first they held open-air meetings in the village square, and in local houses. Then in 1828, they built themselves a small chapel called Bethel on the site of the present building.

It is interesting to see from the photograph (picture 1) that it was brick-built whereas most of the houses of the village are built in stone. The building alongside the Chapel is a bakery.

Increased membership encouraged the Wesleyans to extend the building to twice its size in 1868. In 1924, extensive alterations were made, including the installation of a pipe organ The old bakery was demolished and a new vestry built with a caretaker's flat above.

2. The chapel as it is today

3. The chapel interior

THE CONGREGATIONAL CHAPEL

In 1839, the Congregationalists came to the rapidly growing village. They held services in several private homes until 1845, when they built their own chapel on the lower slopes of Pen-y-Bryn. In 1880, the building became vacant when a new chapel was built on the sea front. It was one of the most attractive buildings in the village.

Built of Penrhyndeudreath stone with Anglesey limestone dressing it has a beautiful window in the front elevation, a spire, and clerestory windows at the side, which is unusual for a chapel. Seating a congregation of 250, it was here that the first harmonium in Aberdyfi was played. This was later replaced with a pipe organ which was the first to be seen and heard in the village. The chapel was closed in 1997.

1. The Congregational Chapel on Pen-y-Bryn

2. The new chapel on the sea front

ST PETER'S CHURCH

The patron saint of much of the land between the Dysyni and Dyfi rivers was Saint Cadfan, to whom the ancient church in Tywyn is dedicated. It was to this church that Aberdyfi people had gone over the years. In 1837, with the growing population, St Peter's church was built. In 1890 a chancel was added, and an organ installed in 1907.

In 1937, the centenary year was commemorated by the installation of new bells in the church tower.

1. Aberdyfi church in 1837. Note the horse and cart and lack of motor cars. The war memorial is absent

2. Bells of Aberdyfi church

3. Later picture of the Aberdyfi church

THE ENGLISH PRESBYTERIAN CHAPEL

The English Presbyterian Chapel was built in 1893 on a site opposite the Literary Institute specifically to cater for the needs of the English-speaking people of the village. The chapel has also become popular over the years with Aberdyfi's many summer visitors.

The chapel shares a minister with the Calvinistic Methodist Chapel.

The English Presbyterian Chapel

THE ROMAN CATHOLIC CHURCH

The Aberdyfi Roman Catholics originally met for worship in a private house called 'Brynderw' on Balkan Hill. In 1931 they moved to the old Methodist Chapel in the Square.

In 1939, a small parcel of land in Penrhos near Neuadd Dyfi was given to the Catholics, together with an old tin hut. This was altered to make a small church. Later it was made larger to cater for the increased membership.

Finally, in 1974 a new church was erected. The grounds were laid out as a garden incorporating a small car park.

The Roman Catholic Church today

6. INTERESTING FEATURES

1. Plaque on cottages in Copper Hill Street

Ann Owen was a wealthy widow and a member of the influential Corbet family of Ynysmaengwyn, Tywyn. They owned much of the land in and around Aberdyfi.

2. Inscription on Dovey Hotel front

The Ship was built in 1729 by Athelstan Corbett of Ynysmaengwyn, Tywyn, as a tavern. It is now known as the Dovey Hotel. This inscription on the Hotel front has the letter N written backwards.

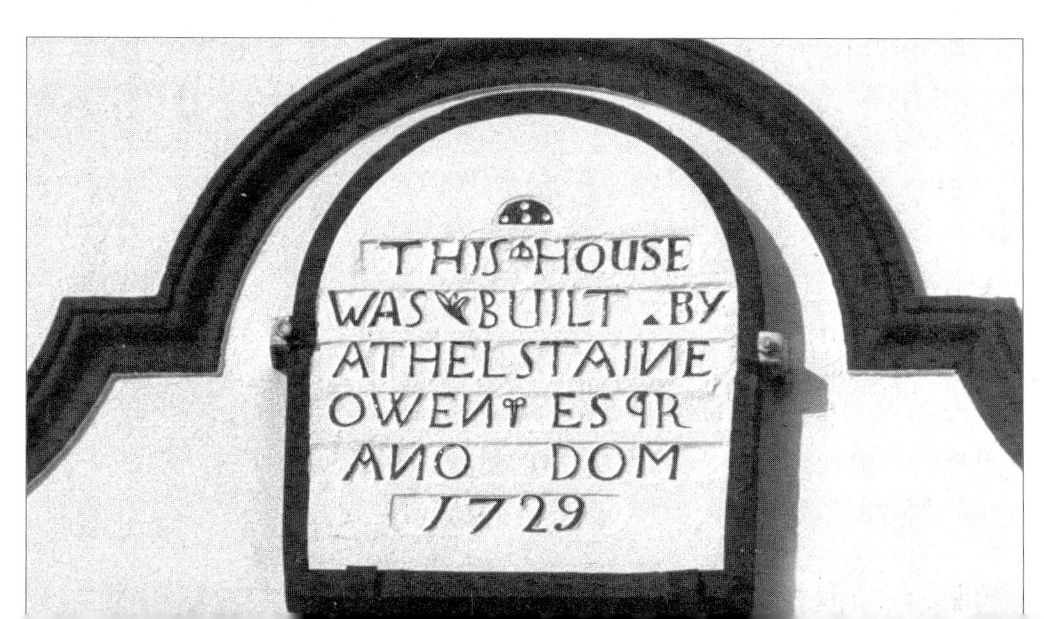

3. Aberdyfi's mythical beast

On the gable-end of a house not far from the Parish Church, stands a little-noticed feature which appears to be some kind of mythical or heraldic bird. On closer inspection it looks more like a griffin or even a dragon. The bird or beast is made of terracotta and clings to the ridge of the roof with its front claws and powerful tail. Its short wings are furled and it carries some kind of ball in its beak.

4. Inscription over the Literary Institute door (1897)

5. Gas lighting: past (1868) and present (1945)

6. Old milestone

7. VILLAGE ACHIEVEMENTS

1972 Prince of Wales Award for Environmental Improvement in Aberdyfi

Presentation by H.R.H. Prince Charles at Denbighshire Technical College

1973 **Winners:** Best Kept Village
Winners: Wales in Bloom
Finalists: Britain in Bloom

Presentation by Sir Alexander Glen, Chairman of the British Tourist Authority, at a special reception in Martini Terrace, London

1974 **Winners**: Best Kept Village

1976 **Winners**: Best Kept Village
Finalists: Wales in Bloom

Presentation by Mr. Barry Jones, M.P., Minister in Charge of Tourism, Welsh Office, at Bangor Normal College

1977 **Winners:** Best Kept Village
Winners: Wales in Bloom
Presentation by Mr. Ednyfed Hudson Davies, Chairman of the Wales Tourist Board, at Swansea Leisure Centre
Finalist: Britain in Bloom
Presentation by Mr. Henry Marking, Chairman of the British Tourist Authority, in London

1978 **Winners:** Best Kept Village
Winners: Wales in Bloom
Presentation at Aberystwyth by Sir Goronwy Daniel, Principal of the University College of Wales
Winners: Britain in Bloom
Presentation by Mrs Alison Munro on behalf of the British Tourist Authority at the Cafe Royal, London

Dinas titles already published:

Aberdyfi: The Past Recalled – Hugh M Lewis £6.95
You Don't Speak Welsh – Sandi Thomas £5.95
Ar Bwys y Ffald – Gwilym Jenkins £7.95
Blodeuwedd – Ogmore Batt £6.95
Black Mountains – David Barnes £6.95
Choose Life! Phyllis Oostermeijer £5.95
Cwpan y Byd a dramâu eraill – J O Evans £4.95
Dragonrise – David Morgan Williams £4.95
The Fizzing Stone – Liz Whittaker £4.95
The Wonders of Dan yr Ogof – Sarah Symons £6.95
Aberdyfi: Past and Present – Hugh M Lewis £6.95
Dysgl Bren a Dysgl Arian – R Elwyn Hughes £9.95

To appear soon:

Clare's Dream – J Gillman Gwynne £4.95
In Garni's Wake – John Rees £7.95
A Dragon To Agincourt – Malcolm Price £6.95
The Dragon Wakes – Jim Wingate £6.95

For a full list of publications, ask for your free copy of our new Catalogue – or simply surf into our secure website, **www.ylolfa.com**, where you may order on-line.

TALYBONT, CEREDIGION, CYMRU (WALES) SY24 5AP
ebost ylolfa@ylolfa.com
gwefan www.ylolfa.com
ffôn (01970) 832 304
ffacs 832 782